My Beautiful Sorrow

Shannon Donovan

authorHOUSE®

AuthorHouse™ UK
1663 Liberty Drive
Bloomington, IN 47403 USA
www.authorhouse.co.uk
Phone: UK TFN: 0800 0148641 (Toll Free inside the UK)
          UK Local: (02) 0369 56322 (+44 20 3695 6322 from outside the UK)

Published by AuthorHouse 06/18/2024

ISBN: 979-8-8230-8783-4 (sc)
ISBN: 979-8-8230-8784-1 (e)

Library of Congress Control Number: 2024910574

Acknowledgement

I dedicate this book to my Nanny Jean.

Someone that inspires me every day to embrace every emotion that I feel and know that it's okay to feel deeply for others. As you always say "love is such sweet sorrow". I take my sensitive soul from you and I wouldn't have it any other way.

I dedicate this book to you because you hold a special place in my heart that no one else can reach.

"Illustrations by Alice Liberty"

The Hearts Asks Pleasure First

The world moved around her
As if floating on air
Every inch of her skin

Consumed by a burning passion
Only living through a dance
Keeping her mind at ease

And as every bad misfortune
Swiftly moved through her
Pleasure took over

The Purpose of Breathing

What makes us human?
The air we breathe?

The body we inhabit our soul in?
The knowledge that we are here and alive?

Yes but what makes us really human?

The way our heart beats
When another soul touches our skin

The emotions that arise
When we get to experience
A pretty sunset or sunrise

The chilling air
That we breathe into our lungs
On those cold winter nights

And the moments that filter your mind
Just as you close your eyes

The answer to the question?

The beautiful, enchanting
Emotions, thoughts and feelings
That we are lucky to experience
Every minute of every single day
For the rest of our lives

Because the way we feel never dies

And yes bodies may age
And yes knowledge may grow distant

But the love felt in our life
That is something else

That will never die

Black and Blue

I wake up
And I see black
As the colour drains from my mind

I grow distant from myself
Nothing is defined boldly

And my eyes close again
As I try to control
Everything that cannot be

But then sometimes
I wake up
And I see blue

I begin to fall gracefully
Into a pool of emotion

My heart beats loudly
And my face
Covered in colour

As I release
All the blue
That left me on those black days

And my true soul finally greets me again

Oblivion

She does not care for money
Or for tradition

She only cares for attraction
Connection
A true interaction

With no falsely led intentions
Or future endeavours

Just present spontaneity
And moments of really living

She takes up your thoughts
She absorbs your purpose to live
And she inspires passion, love and all things desired

So embrace her
Allow her radiation of light in her life
To fill yours

Whatever Happens Tomorrow, We Had Today

Living on a dream
A moment of ecstasy
So bitter yet so sweet

An intense feeling
Like no one else can fathom
Or begin to imagine

Every word that they breathe
And every move that they make

As their hand wraps around my waist
Their head buried into my chest
As my heart aches in silent happiness

And these moments pass me
As quickly as they come

No one makes me as sad
Or as content

Give me just one day
One day is all that is needed
With the light in my life

The Melody Sways

Oh to be able to taste
The beauty that flows
From the words of a song

Each line innocently dancing
To its own beat

Unaware of its impact
On the lives of so many

Our ears are filled
With the sounds of pure emotion

As we feel ourselves falling
Losing sight of reality
And grasping onto imaginary

Those overwhelming ballads
Those mellow notes

Those aching pauses
That bring us the most pain
Yet the most happiness

The Pier

I witness birds

Flowing through the air gracefully
Their wings spread wide

And their beauty filtered
Across the light blue sky

And all I see is you

I witness sand

The delicate yet rough touch
That it presents

That makes your toes curl
In the most satisfying way

And still all I see is you

I witness the ocean

It's deep complexity
Yet electrifying violence

As the waves crash relentlessly

Against each other
And yet all I see is you

I witness the lighthouse

Shining its light across the horizon
In the most dazzling way

Standing the test of time
Amongst the rocky shore

And all I see is you

I witness the pier

That I stand upon
It's historical value

That captures it's essence
So magically

As I turn
And all I see is you

Honeymoon Decadence

What is now the norm
Was once the new

What is now the old
Was once the bold

The demise of the flame of passion
But the attachment that still remains

The loss of new beginnings
But the gain of an eternity-lasting companion

Not just a lover
But in fact a best friend

Through thick and thin
Through bad and good
Through ugly and pretty

Forever intertwined
In memories of a lifetime

For better or for worse
In sickness and in health

Till the last breath is finally taken

The Rollercoaster of Trauma

How we allow ourselves
To be immersed within
The depths of raw emotion
Caused from the actions of another
Is both magical and frightening

How can heartache be so appealing?
The strength of its development
As it grows
To form an overbearing height

One in which we are both intrigued
And intimidated by

The captivation of no longer being in control
As you enjoy the ride

Speechless and unable to move
Formed on the basis
Of someone else's power

And yet we thrive from it
Enjoying every peak
And embracing every dangerous fall

Daisies

Young and carefree
Blowing in the wind

You enter my world
Plucking each singular petal
Like it means nothing

Do you love me?
Do you love me not?

You leave me completely bare
As I watch you
Carelessly taking my beauty

My confidence and pride
My all the time happiness

And yet you gain nothing from this
Only entitlement to my broken heart

Not Waving, But Drowning

The beaming rays of innocence
Shine down on our skin

As we fully embrace
Every splash of water
That we encounter

A harmless comment
A passing thought

A gaze across a busy room
A moment of deafening silence

Whilst the deep darkness of the ocean
Envelopes our complex minds

We experience somewhat of an illusion:

We perceive independence
Yet are screaming out for support

We promote optimism
Yet our thoughts are cruel

We encourage strength within
Yet imperfect weakness
Protrudes out of our bodies
We are waving in happiness
Yet drowning in sorrow

And still we continue this cycle
Allowing our real voices
To fall to the bottom of the ocean

Internally we are muted and unheard
Externally our actions are misconstrued
To what we want people to see

Because in fact
We are not waving
But drowning

An Emotional Craving

Why is it that we crave it so much?
This one feeling
Described in so many ways
With so many different depths

One word, one touch, one look
Accounts for this indescribable emotion

We feel this need for having it in our lives
Because without it?
We would be lost

It makes us feel sick
Unable to speak

But the safety and convenience we receive from it
Is now too easy to have

We live for it
And we forget everything

Simply because we have love in our life

Buzz of New Beginnings

First encounters
The nerves and excitement

Wrapped into these little moments
Only room for appreciation and admiration

Learning to understand each other
The boundaries, the interests
And everything in between

Drunk on the little touches
The laughs had and the moments shared

The start of something beautiful

Food for Thought

A cycle so vicious
To be released from it would be heaven

Dark and twisted thoughts
My mind imploding

On what was once loved so dearly
And is now seen as a crime

I now spend my nights
Waiting for the perfect moment
To "have a shower" or "go to the bathroom"

Silently sobbing into my pillow that same night
Regretting all of my actions
Praying to God no one hears me

I have become someone I don't know anymore

Will I ever be free from it?
No

But I will learn from it
And embrace every bodily curve

My Caladium

Like an angel sent from up above
You fill my world with light and love

What a beautiful sight it was to see
So strong
So brave
So carefree

You made me want to be
A better version of me

Your soul could light up
An entire city

And you don't even know it
So innocent
So pretty

Forever in my life
My Caladium

Feels Like Home

I wasn't ready for another heartache
I wasn't ready to be told more lies

All this doubt and fear
Enveloping in my mind

My own fear was stopping me

And what I didn't realise
Was that I was drawn

To someone so beautiful in every way

From the pure kind nature that they embody
Down to the safety and security that they bring

How they could love me in their whole entirety
And I finally felt like home

Like shattered glass repaired
My smiles becoming more frequent

And my life starting again

As if evolving from the darkest place
And I finally felt like home

And whilst I continue to wonder how I got so lucky
You look into my eyes

And make me forget why I ever worried before
About not feeling enough

I have found my happy place
With the soul that makes me feel alive

And it feels like home

Another Love

It is hard to believe
That we have the capacity
To feel love again

We were so attached
So invested
So in awe

Of that one person

God forbid we could love another
In the same way

But it happens
We allow the darkness that person brought
When they left our lives

To be filled
By the light that the good people emanate

And we fully embrace what will be

Prom Queen

Judgement - always
Expectations - high

Comparisons - endless
Self love - damaged

Overthinking - present
Mind games - cruel

Happiness - strained
Love - complicated

Beauty - flawed
Pain - inflicted

Consequences - scary
Life - a vicious cycle

Right Person, Wrong Time

I've never really believed
In what you would call
Right person, wrong time

Why?

Because it seemed like such an easy way
To deflect the truth that they were just
Simply the wrong person for you

But after experiencing love in its truest form
It all makes sense to me now

That there are people you meet in your life

Some that stay forever
And some that you have to let go
Regardless of the depth of your feelings

Whether they were your great love

Or simply a passing thought
A distant memory

It feels like such a waste
So much energy and time spent on a person
You thought would be your forever
But was never destined to be

Maybe we did meet too soon

Maybe if we had met years from now
The timing would have been perfect

And external factors
Wouldn't have impacted the love that we shared
The love that we built

Trauma may have been healed
Growth may have been reached

We would be at peace with our past
And our happiness would have been prominent

But unfortunately you can't choose the timing

Our journey in love may have never ended
With the right person at the right time

But sadly that part isn't up to us
When you meet the right person at the wrong time

The Night Owl

She sits in her room staring at the blank canvas
Thinking of all of the possibilities

Wondering whether anything would be more beautiful
Than those stars in the sky
-
As she starts to question things...

Why is the air that we breathe
So much more exhilarating at night?

How can the deafening silence with only murmurs heard
Make you feel so warm inside?

Can the sound of rain in sunlight
Make you fall into a trance like it does in moonlight?

Why is stillness so effortlessly perfect
When bodies are hibernating?

How can the thrill of a late night drive
Fill our hearts with joy more so than any other time?

These questions may not be answered
But she was sure that she would be forever in paradise
As she sits in her room staring at the sky
Thinking of all the possibilities

Love In Its Purest Form

A small fire ignites inside
As we drown into each others eyes

Lips pressed
Bodies intertwined

An innocence embodied through our smiles
Butterflies of excitement fill up the room

An almost powerful and powerless feeling
Fulfilling each other with every touch

Until there's nothing left to give
Collapsing into one

A calm and warm presence
Filling up the space

A silent happiness

Bittersweet Symphony

There's a feeling unlike any other
When you are completely at peace

In this little moment of ecstasy
Hard to explain but easy to forget

Until life breaks you down again

That feeling will always come back though
Unexpectedly and unexplainably perfect

Like when you find that perfect song
And it could be played on repeat for hours

But the realisation that that initial feeling will fade
And the music will become monotonous
Like every other song before

A bittersweet symphony

The Unbreakable Bond

A ferocious urge to protect
After years of witnessing pain, tears, misery and silence

A forever kind of care
Past, present and future loyalty

Without any need to doubt
That it's not reciprocated back

To love someone in their entirety
Knowing that they appreciate you
For who you truly are

Having a best friend, counsellor, sister and role model
All in one

It's the Unbreakable bond

Mother and daughter

Take a Bow

Let's put on a show
You'll hide those insecurities
You didn't have

Put on that mask
As you step onto the big stage
And perform a spectacular show

So go ahead and take a bow

Let's protrude greatness
But a fake greatness

One that doesn't really exist
To make others see you
As complete perfection

But it doesn't work this time does it?

All the lies
Breaking through the surface

But go ahead and take a bow

Why not play victim forever
And pretend that none of this
Was ever your fault
And everyone is impacted by this

Not just the magicians assistant
But the audience too

Watching it all unfold
So go ahead

The mastermind behind the show

Take a bow

Strawberries and Cream

Walking up to the door
As the smell of fir trees reach my nose

Heading straight for the sliding back door
As the blazing sun overlooks the garden wall

Those buzzing bees and vibrant flowers
Intertwined along the walls

Fresh laundry drying in the breeze
As the dream catcher sings

Indulging in my bowl
Of strawberries and cream

A memory of nostalgia
Engrained in my mind forever

I'll never forget

The bowl of strawberries and cream

Barbie

Living in this lost world
No sense of purpose

A lack of understanding
What was I made for?

Perfect skin, perfect hair
Perfect face, perfect body

A perfect life.

It never is though

No matter how hard
You strive for perfect

It will never be
Completely perfect

No appreciation
For mistakes, flaws

The honest reality of life

Just expectations
Extremely high expectations
Of a real life Barbie

Wicked Game

The never ending feeling of pain
As the giant ball rises up into my throat

Spiralling into an epitome of low
How can love be so cruel?

I watch as you take my soul, my mind, my everything,
my nothing

Will I ever survive this cruel game we play?

Lifeless

I look at myself and see someone else
A distant once upon a time

Where eyes were vibrant
Are now dull

My skin full of colour
And now a snowy white

My body untouchable
To now unlovable

Who am I?
Where did I go?

Prey to the Predator

Eyes full of fear
As I step out into the unknown

My mouth opens but nothing comes out
Waiting for the right time to enter home

Before the predator wakes

But one snap of a twig
Or a crunch of a leaf
And my fate is sealed

The roars begin to rip
Through all the noise

As I await my inevitable position

Of prey to the predator

The Eternal City

The cobbled streets surround me

As I wander down a dimly lit street

To find my way home

My eyes passing over the ancient buildings

showcasing the beauty of a hands work

The bakeries all closed for the night

As the familiar smell of cheese and tomato fill the air

The hustle and bustle begins to rise

As the sound of live music rushes through my veins

And I notice the people of the city

The young lovers with hands intertwined

Eyes locked and smiles synchronised

As they dance into the night

The familiar lady and her designated bench

Tilting her head as if on her late husband's shoulder

Remembering the days

Of what used to be

There in the bright moonlight

Stood the eternal city

In all of its glory

In Another Life

Sometimes I think about what could have been

I tried so hard to protect you from this world
With every fibre in my being

All your troubles and past traumas
But sometimes that's not enough

Maybe in another world
I didn't need to do that

Maybe just maybe
You would have healed from all of that

And I never would have had to worry
About not being enough for you

Maybe we could have been happy
Our lives could have intertwined

And nothing could have got in our way
Nothing would have broken us down

No feelings of anger or hatred towards the world

Just peace and serenity
In our own little bubble
But the bubble burst in this life
As I desperately tried to get it back
Pushing the obvious aside

But once a bubble is burst
There is no way to save it

The imaginary bubble still remains
In the unspoken corners of my mind

And I can live with that
Knowing what we could have been

In another life

Butterflies in the Garden

Our passion
Like a burning flame

This undeniable electricity
As you reach for my hand
And I melt at your side

You take all of me
As do I to you

Your lips brush mine
And my heart starts to race

And those butterflies in the garden
Will never leave

I'll love you until the end of time

The Beauty of Physical Touch

I love the little touches

To others they may seem insignificant
But simple gestures of affection
Can be electrifying for me

A hand around my waist
Grazing their fingers up and down my arm
Resting their head on my shoulder
Running their fingers through my hair

A kiss on the shoulder
A squeeze of my hand

There's something so calming about it
It makes you feel at ease
Content within that fleeting moment

The beauty of physical touch

You Need Somebody Too

"Let's not talk about me"
"What's been going on with you?"

"I've spoken too much."
"How are you feeling?"

"Oh I'll be alright!"
"Are you going to be okay?"

"I'm actually doing fine."
"How are you coping with everything?"

"I don't need anybody."

No you need somebody too...

Lost at Sea

Like a distant shadow
I can see your face
Calling out to me at sea
Struggling to breathe

Oh how I ache to understand
The crash of every wave that hits

The rise and fall
Of the water surrounding you

If I could take every moment of pain
Every sharp inhale of breath
Every painful release

I wouldn't flinch
I would take it all

In a minute
In a heartbeat
In a second

And if I can't take your place
Let me drown with you

As we both sink
To the bottom of the ocean

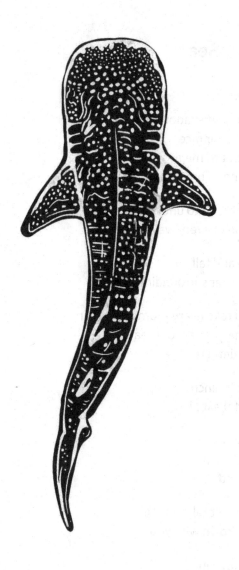

If Only

In some other world
A different universe

I meet my mum
Only 16 years old

Not another soul purer
So beautifully young

We would have laughed forever
Filled the world with our love

And danced the night away
Unconditional fun

Watching her happiness
Fill the room

Like a shining light
Such a free spirit
What a captivating sight

I would distract her if I could
As we would run down the street

Singing at the top of our lungs
And leave that place behind
Let her forget about the boy
With those brown, gazing eyes

I wouldn't have to worry
About her eventual demise

The day her world
Would change forever

The day my dad arrived

It Takes Two to Tango

Feeling too much yet feeling nothing
All at the same time

An explosion of emotions
Soaring through my body

Till the point of exhaustion arrives
But not for long

As this beautiful dance never ends
With the partner of my life

It feels like I've nearly made it out
And then there you are

Standing right in front of me

You extend your hand
And ask me for another dance

And my heart melts
All over again

Who Knows

I always wonder
If I would have ever felt this way

If you had kept me safe from the world
Like I always thought you would

If you had reassured me
That everything was going to be okay

If you hadn't been so wrapped up
In your own emotions

And stopped for a minute in your chaotic life
And thought about me

The supposed light in your life
Your little girl
The apple to your eye

Would I have felt less reliant
On everyone else making me happy.

Would I have finally felt good enough?

Maybe, maybe not
Who knows...

My Garden

How exhausting it is
To be everything for everyone
All at once

The storm fogs up my brain and the pressure builds
As I work day and night in my garden

Seed after seed sown in the soil
My own happiness
Jeopardised for the love that I feel for others

My mind doesn't stop
It's like a merry go round

Giving out all the flowers in my garden
Until one singular rose remains

I look down at what's left and weep until it hurts

A moment of weakness
Which then falls into silence

And I realise that my garden is not empty

The bodies surrounding my garden
Take each others hands
And help my flowers grow again

The grass becomes greener
As the sunshine beams over the horizon

And I finally realise
How amazing it is

To be everything for everyone
All at once

Life Support

When you need me
Not when I need you

You pour your heart out on the floor
Leaving me to pick up the remnants
Of your distant happiness

I will forever be the slave to your heart
Your life support

Beautiful Scars

That inevitable gut wrenching feeling
When your stomach drops

As you come to the realisation
That they didn't live up to the expectations
You placed on them

You put them up on this pedestal
And allow them to absorb your whole world

And then they scar you, bit by bit
Every poor word choice that they make
Every action they exert

That makes you question whether
They truly want to be a part of your world

And it all comes down to how much you can take
How much impact it has on your self worth
And how you value yourself

It is crazy to think
That we can allow another person
To determine whether we are enough for others

And what makes us less special to another
Comparing and analysing and overthinking
When in reality
We are inevitably in control of our lives

People within our lives are a factor
A chapter, an element
Some may say an added bonus

This means they are not central to you
And they never will be

You are always the centre of your own life

And reflecting this out into the world
Is what will bring you true happiness

What Once Was

Looking back at memories
Old videos from when we were kids

I don't think we'll ever be
What we once were

Never ashamed of being silly with each other
Always laughing for no reason

Watching our favourite films like Good Burger
and Aliens in the Attic

You'll forget when you called me your Shannon
And would never be afraid to tell me what was wrong

And I'll forget when I came into your room
To reassure you not to worry about the argument
downstairs

Me being there for you when mum was mad
And you being there for me when dad made me cry

As the years have gone by
We may have lost those moments together

Yet despite all of that I know deep down

We will always understand each others hurt
And protect each other till the end of time

Because you're my baby brother
And I'm your big sister
And nothing will ever change that

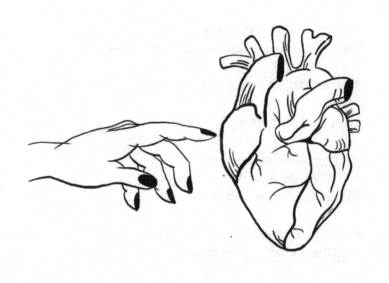

It's Not Her

Her happiness radiates every room
And you know that

You see the way people look at her
The way people are captivated by her presence

Because that's how you feel

And yet all she sees is you

She loves love
And when she finds it
She pours her heart out on the floor

And gives you everything that she can
Until there's nothing left to give

It's like the intensity and realness
That she brings to the relationship

Scares you so much
And you know that

You will try to find that same feeling
In every other woman you meet

Every encounter
Every experience
Every moment

Through the looks in someone's eyes
Through the smiles created from laughter
Through the way they caress their hand with yours

But it won't be the same will it

Because it won't be her eyes
Her smile
Her hand

It's not her
Not anymore

And that's what you must live with

The beauty of what you had
In the grasp of your hands

But you let it slip

Daffodils

The first flower to bloom in spring

Signifying the end of cold dark days

Known to survive anything

That's what you are to me

Someone who has so much strength

That they will put others first

Ahead of themselves

You brighten up so many people's worlds

And you don't even realise it

Your energy and happiness

Inspires me to be a better person

I'm so lucky to have found you

To call you my best friend

Our friendship stands the test of time

Just like daffodils

Stand through every season

To Love and Be Loved

The great true love
That people pray for

Wish they get to experience
Just one time on this earth

And I have
In its complete entirety

Being completely consumed by someone

Every memory
Every moment

Their eyes and smile

Finding comfort
In their hugs and kisses

The reassuring gestures of affection
Lighting up my world

I find the greatest joy in the little things
A touch, a look, a smile, a laugh

And I can finally feel my heart
Coming back completely

I know how it feels to love and be loved
No more unrequited one sided agony

My first thought and always my last
I appreciate every inch of their existence in my world

My Safe Haven

There's something so special
About the love shared
Between grandparents
And their grandchildren

It's almost as if it's an entirely
Different kind of love

There's never any malicious intent
To cause any pain

Wanting the best for you
In every aspect of your life

They'll always be your biggest supporter
Through everything

Nothing makes them love you less
But everything makes them love you more

You can talk about your biggest fears
Or your scariest thoughts
And they will really listen to you

They will respond with kindness and wisdom
Getting a completely different perspective on life

Hearing stories from when they were young
All the great memories made
And it warms your heart

They crave those little moments with you
Coming round for a cup of tea and a chat
Makes their entire day
They enjoy every minute they get to spend with you

There's nothing I could be more grateful for
Than to have experienced this love in my life

The best kind of love that there is

My safe haven

Just One night

The cold night air
Fills my lungs

As you take my hand
And lead the way

A breathtaking view
Yet you take my breath away

Your touch exhilarates me
You make me feel alive

All I needed was one night with you

Nothing more
Nothing Less

Satisfied with your calming presence
Comfortable and content

Passion and intensity
Fills the room

That is all I craved
When I was with you

No expectations
No judgement

Just peace
And complete serenity

That's what you have given me

In just one night

Oxymoron

I love love
It's a shame it hurts so much when it tries to leave

But you can't force love to stay
When it will only turn to hate

Happy moments turn to distant memories
And I find peace in that

Something that is now once was
The oxymoron of life

Platonic Soulmates

There are only a few people in this world
That make you feel complete

Through honesty and loyalty
As a friend

People that will give you everything
Love in its simplest form

When they find peace in your happiness
Being met with empathy and understanding

Will never stop loving you
Through your ups and downs

And help you out of the darkness
Letting you shine once again

When you find that in people
Don't let them go

Because platonic soulmates are for life

Intoxicating

Head is spinning
I've lost control
Taking me away from my reality

Everything seems brighter
A little bit better

My body relaxes and I feel present
In the moment
With the people that matter most

My anxiety fades
Now only protruding confidence
My happiness is prominent

An intoxicating yet thrilling feeling

La Dolce Far Niente

Sometimes I wish I could move away somewhere
I'd live by the coast

A place that doesn't require me to be perfect
Because the place itself already is

I can eat good food and not be judged

I can spend all day reading a book
With no worries in the world

Just effortless happiness
Content with my purpose on earth

To enjoy the present
In order to fulfil my future

The sweetness of doing nothing

Lover Girl

She's just a girl who wants to be loved

No grand gestures
Just genuine love

Simple love
Gentle love

We give that to someone
And they absorb it

So much to the point
That they forget how special it is
To be loved like that

They take advantage of that love

Rely on it
Get comfortable with it
Breaking it down slowly over time

Comforting us with lies
Only to be hurt by the truth

We get ripped apart
But all we do is care
Care so deeply that it hurts

We will do everything in our power
To love someone with every
Fibre in our being

Yet we are always the ones that get hurt

Embrace or Destroy

Your heart is big
Your love is unconditional

And you're not afraid to express it

No matter what you go through
You won't let that side of yourself diminish

You'll just be consistent in who deserves to witness it
To live in it every day

Because what good is your big heart
If it's made to feel small

And what is the point in unconditional
When it's unrequited

There is a beauty in this pain though
Suffering drives us deeper
And makes us kinder

Gives us an understanding of other people's pain

So either learn to embrace it
Or let it destroy you

About the Author

Shannon is a young published author of My Beautiful Sorrow who always dreamed of being an author when she was a little girl. She has always been inspired by poetry and the beauty of words and how they can capture an experience, a life, a loss, a love. She is passionate about encouraging people to embrace what life throws at you.